Seven Aspects

of

Salvation

Brian Sherring

ISBN: 978-1-78364-209-0

www.obt.org.uk

****

The Open Bible Trust
Fordland Mount, Upper Basildon,
Reading, RG8 8LU, GB.

Seven Aspects of Salvation

Contents

1. Introduction

When I was a young Christian I worked with a Nurses Christian Fellowship in a local hospital; an enthusiastic and committed group of people who held services in some of its wards and were not ashamed to speak to patients and staff about their faith. (Today, that practice, thanks to the PC Brigade who seem bent on destroying the last vestiges of common sense, is banned in many places.) In that environment, a person on becoming a Christian, was expected to witness to that fact before a congregation, saying why they had become so and the circumstances that led up to it; it was known as 'their testimony'. I suppose it was based upon the words of Paul in Romans 10:9,

> If you shall *confess with your mouth* the Lord Jesus, and shall *believe in your heart* that God has raised Him from the dead, you shall be saved.

And the burning question that was asked of congregations and individuals was, 'are you saved?' And if you claimed you were then, 'have you given your testimony yet?' It was all so black and white, so simple.

When later I began to devote more of my time to the study of the Scriptures, I realised that whilst the one act of faith in Christ was enough to secure a person's 'salvation', included within the word was a complex series of aspects that touched every part of a Christian's life. In this series of chapters, I consider them under seven heads:

- Identification,
- Reconciliation,
- Redemption,
- Justification,
- Atonement,
- Sanctification and
- *Aionian* Life.

Together they sum up a person's need and God's remedy in Christ. They are like the seven colours of the rainbow that exist separately, but when brought together add up to the brilliance of white light. 'Salvation is God's 'white light'; the different colours the seven aspects that come together to help us to see the complete picture.

In the *Interpreter's Dictionary of the Bible*, A. Richardson wrote: "Salvation is the central theme of the whole Bible, and as such is related to every other biblical theme". It is a vast subject, and biblically encompasses the whole of life, as we know it. It is not enough to see it like a man who jumps into a river and saves someone drowning, only to abandon him or her on the bank to get on with it; it is to be saved *from* and to be saved *to*. The new life in Christ that it brings is expressed in various ways in the writings of the three apostles:

- John: John's Gospel 3:3, 8: born again (or from above) ... born of the Spirit.
- Paul: 2 Corinthians 5:17: If anyone is in Christ he is a new creation.
- Peter: 2 Peter 1:4: May become partakers of the divine nature.

Salvation in the Scriptures is both individual and

national. In the ancient world, salvation encompassed the whole of life. It included survival and deliverance from enemies, and the peace and freedom that followed. In the case of the people of Israel, they could look back to their deliverance as a nation from Egypt under Moses, a 'fact' of which they were constantly reminded. Their God was "The Lord your God *who brought you out of the land of Egypt*". But He was also the God who was ready to take them into the Promised Land, had their faith been sufficient to grasp it. And this reminds us that there is a practical side to salvation. Their redemption could not be undone, but there were "things that belong to (accompany) salvation" (Hebrews 6:9).

The seven words that make up 'salvation' are being presented in this series in an order in which I believe it is convenient to consider them. I am not suggesting that they happen in that order. Although this is to some degree how they are presented to us in the Scriptures. For example, the first of those words, 'identification', is the first aspect that is brought before us when God created man (male and female): "God created man in *the likeness of his own image*" (Genesis 1:27); man as created, was 'identified' with God. And, after sin is dealt with in Christ, as John wrote, "We know that when he appears *we shall be like Him*, because we shall see Him as He is" (1 John 3:2)—identified with Christ.

But Paul refers to a much more complex aspect of "identification' in Romans 5:12-21, where he sees mankind as both 'identified' with Adam and his death, and 'identified' with Christ and His life. In terms of resurrection this is expressed as, "As in Adam all die, so also in Christ we shall all be made alive" (1 Corinthians 15:22). Identification with God in Christ is both His intention and the goal of salvation.

As far as God's earthly purpose is concerned, the stewardship of that salvation was committed to Israel—" Salvation is from the Jews" (John 4:22). When they failed to fulfil that responsibility, rejecting the Messiah who had made possible the salvation of all mankind by His death on the cross and resurrection from the dead, God's salvation was sent to the Gentiles, and His purpose for the earth through that people was put on hold (Acts 28:25-28) Today we Gentiles rejoice in a 'salvation' that encompasses "spiritual blessings in heavenly places" as set out in Ephesians 1:3-14. Out future is no longer bound up with Israel on earth, and a relationship to the seed of Abraham. The faith of Abraham, however, that led to his being "justified by faith", is still *an example* for all people in whatever calling, and this fact must form part of our consideration of that aspect of salvation, as we "look to Jesus, the founder and perfector of our faith" (Hebrews 12:2).

2. Identification: A Goal

Identification may be looked at from two angles, as God's original intention and goal for mankind, the subject of this current chapter, and identification put into practice in our Christian lives, to be dealt with in the next chapter, In the first it is the contrast between identification with Adam and identification with Christ, expressed in the context of resurrection as, "*in Adam* all die ... *in Christ* shall all be made alive" (1 Corinthians 15:22) In the second it is the practical outcome of identification with Christ here and now.

The concept of identification in the Scriptures is the first 'fact' associated with the creation and goal of humanity. God determined that our first parents, as archetypes of mankind as a whole, were to be "made in *the likeness* of the image of God" (Genesis 1:26, 27 *The Companion Bible*). Interrupted by the entrance of sin and death into man's environment, that object continues to be a 'fact' that has now been made possible by Jesus Christ and His one great sacrifice. For as both Paul and John state:

> Just as we have born the image of the man of dust [Adam], *so shall we also bear the image of the man from heaven* [Christ]. (1 Corinthians 15:49)

> We know that when he appears *we shall be like Him*, because we shall see Him as He is. (1 John 3:2)

But Paul takes us deeper into the 'mechanics' of identification in Romans 5:11-21, where he speaks of identification as being "in Adam" and "in Christ", as the basis upon which reconciliation to God is built. He writes of,

> Our Lord Jesus Christ, through whom we have now received the *reconciliation. On this account (dia touto)* as through one man … death through sin ... so also through one (man) ... righteousness that leads to justification of life. (lit.)

By Christ's one act of righteousness, reconciliation has dealt with man's alienation from God brought about through Adam's one act of disobedience, and that has been accomplished through 'identification'. Here we have three aspects of salvation brought together that demonstrate that whilst we may consider them apart for ease of study, they are part of one great whole:

Identification, Reconciliation, Justification of life.

Romans 5:12-21 is difficult enough to read, let alone expound! Paul enters upon his subject, only to be side-tracked by introducing the law into the equation, and then he returns to the original subject later. To try and make this passage easier to read, some versions have introduced brackets into the text (*KJV*), or at least a long dash, 'em' (*English Standard Version*). In a short chapter this passage cannot be considered in great detail, but see my book *Paul's Letter to the Romans: Background and Introduction* (published by The Open Bible Trust)

The key feature of this passage is 'identification'—identification with Adam and his sin and identification with Christ and His righteousness. The word 'one' occurs 12 times here in 10 verses but the words 'faith/believe' are absent. The nearest we get to faith in this passage is in the phrase, "they which receive" (17). Faith is not involved until there is something to "receive". As we shall see that which has to be received is 'reconciliation'.

There is a deeper concept of identification in Romans 5:12-21 than simply 'likeness'. Adam is "the "figure (*tupos* 'type') of Him that was to come (Christ)" (14) but in an opposite (antithetical) sense. The comparison is between the negative and the positive. However, if 'identification' is to be a reality then:

> Since therefore the children share in flesh and blood, *He Himself likewise partook of the same things*, that through death He might destroy the one who has the power of death, that is the devil, and deliver all those who through fear of death were subject to

lifelong slavery. (Hebrews 2:14, 15 see verse17; John 1:14; Romans 8:3)

Christ, to effect salvation for mankind, had first to *identify* Himself with mankind—" born in the likeness of men... found in human form" (Philippians 2:7,8). The book of Ruth, where Boaz, Ruth's 'kinsman', redeems her inheritance, is a picture book that illustrates that to redeem in ancient Israel, one had to be 'a kinsman'. And so it was with Jesus.

Adam then was a type of Christ, who is "the last Adam" and "the second man" (1 Corinthians 15:45, 47). As such they both stand identified with mankind, the one bequeathing sin and death, the other bringing life and righteousness. "All men" are involved in Adam's sin and death, as they are in Christ's one act that brought "justification of life" (5:18). More on this in the following chapters.

3. Identification: Practical Living

In the last chapter I dealt with the 'fact' of identification with Christ, ending with Paul's words in Romans 5:18:

> As the trespass of one (Adam) led to condemnation for all men, so the act of righteousness of one (Christ) leads to justification of life for all men.

I have pointed out that the words 'faith' and 'believe' do not appear in Paul's arguments in the context of this statement; that is because he is speaking of "all men", not just believers, for whom Christ has given "justification of life". To understand this fully, we have to consider Paul's argument in this passage (5:12-21), that looks back to Adam and the entry of sin and death. Adam was told concerning the tree of the knowledge of good and evil, "*In the day* that you eat of it *you shall surely die*" (Genesis 2:17). Not, 'may die' or even 'fail to a thousand years' (he lived to 930!), but, "*surely* die". Taking the word 'day' to mean 24 hours, as it has been used throughout the preceding record in Genesis, why did God not *apparently* keep His word? I believe it was because the sacrifice of Christ is just as effective for those who have lived as it is for those who now live, or will live in the future. And that sacrifice gives, "justification of life *for all men*". And it justified a continuation of life for Adam, and allowed his life to proceed beyond "the day that you eat thereof ..."

Identification "in Christ" also guarantees all a resurrection: "For as by a man came death, by a man has come also the resurrection of the dead. For as in Adam *all die*, so also in Christ *all shall be made alive*". (1 Corinthians 15:21, 22). This passage says nothing here about the fate of the "all", it simply makes the point that all die in Adam and all are made alive in Christ. (For more on the resurrections in Scripture see Michael and Sylvia Penny's booklet, *Resurrection: When?*)

The words, "*In (God), we* live and move and

have our being" is applied by Paul to the idolaters in Athens of the present life in Acts 17:28. But of course, whether we believe this and *how* we live our lives is another matter. And the Christian's response to this truth is likely be very different from that of an unbeliever.

Identified with Christ: The practical outcome

The concept of identification in Christ provides a springboard from which the believer's life can be lived out according to God's will. In Romans 5:12-21 Paul speaks not just of life but also of "reigning in life" (verses 17, 21). Reigning is over and above living as can be seen in 2 Timothy 2:11-13:

If we have *died* with Him, we will also *live* with Him;
if we endure, we will *also reign* with Him;
If we deny Him, He will also deny us;
if we are faithless, He remains faithful—
for He cannot deny Himself.

To die with Him and to live with Him is seen here as an accomplished fact by the sacrifice of Christ, a position that is not at risk and cannot be forfeited, for He cannot deny Himself, but it does not guarantee a reward; that will be denied if we are faithless. So in Romans 5:12-21, working from the premise that identification with Christ is an accomplished fact, Paul moves on in the next chapter and translates this fact into practical living, a life that will bring its reward: "You must *consider yourselves* dead to sin and alive to God in Christ Jesus" (verse 11).

"Consider" is the Greek *logizomai*, used of Abraham who, "believed God, and it was *counted* to Him as righteousness". What Paul is saying here is effectively, if you believe you are *identified with Christ* in His death—**reckon it to be so**. Take hold of it and let that knowledge become a reality in your Christian life. The logic behind it is, "How can we who died to sin still live in it?" (6:2). You are living in a different environment, you cannot live in the old one any more. In the writings of Paul we find him detailing our identification with Christ in seven steps, five in Romans during the Acts period, plus two in Ephesians where he is referring to the Church which is the Body of Christ, whose hope is in "the heavenly places" (1:3).

- Crucified **with Him** (6:6).
- Dead **with Him** (6:8).
- Buried **with Him** (6:4).
- Quickened **with Him** (8:11 *KJV*).
- Raised **with Him** (6:5).

This is far as the Acts period takes us. When we come to the Church, the Body of Christ, we can add,

- Raised up (ascended) **with Him**.
- Seated **with Him** in the heavenly places" (Ephesians 2:6).

But this is to anticipate the goal of identification; we have yet to consider those other aspects that go to make up the "mechanics" of salvation. And we will begin with reconciliation which Paul links in Romans 5:11 with identification in Adam and Christ in verses 12 to 21:

We rejoice in God through our Lord Jesus Christ, through whom we have now received reconciliation. *On account of this* ... (identification) through Adam ... through Jesus Christ our Lord.

In the next chapter, reconciliation is seen as both national, in the case of Israel, and individual in its connection with all men. And Paul makes a connection between the two which led to the calling of Gentiles during that period. Paul wrote: "Through (Israel's) trespass salvation has come to the Gentiles, so as to make Israel jealous ... *their rejection means the reconciliation of the world*" (11:11, 15). And we must also remember that the word 'reconciliation' implies a division between two parties. Reconciliation with God is **for** all men, but they are called upon to "receive the reconciliation".

4. Reconciliation

The very mention of the word 'reconciliation' suggests that a 'difference' has taken place between two parties that has now been 'healed'. That 'difference' may have been originally caused by a word, an action, a disagreement or even a religious belief. And it may have been trifling or serious. 'Differences' can lead to married people becoming divorced, neighbours going to law, even nations waging war with each other. But the most serious 'difference' of all is that which existed between God and man. Whilst in human affairs there is often blame on both sides, in this case all the blame lies with man. So serious was the difference between God and man that Paul referred to the latter as "enemies" of God (Romans 5:10). But he spoke of it in a context of love and hope:

> God shows his love for us in that *while we were still sinners, Christ died for us* ... we have now been justified by his blood ... saved from the wrath of God. For if *while*

we were enemies we were reconciled to God by the death of his Son, much more, now that we are reconciled, shall we be saved by his life. (5:8-10)

Reconciliation involves two parties; here it is God and man. The "death of God's Son" has destroyed that enmity and made reconciliation possible. Nothing now stands between Him and mankind. But reconciliation is two-way. It may be that in a human situation one or other of the two parties at enmity might relent and be prepared to be reconciled to the other. But for that reconciliation to be a reality 'it takes two'. Reconciliation between God and man is likewise. On God's part, the alienation between God and man has been broken down in Christ, but to be effective for the individual, reconciliation *has to be received*. In 2 Corinthians 5:18 Paul refers to his ministry as "the ministry of reconciliation", and he goes on to describe it:

In Christ God was reconciling the world to Himself, not counting their trespasses against them, and entrusting to us the message of reconciliation. Therefore, we are ambassadors for Christ, God making his appeal through us. **We implore you on behalf of Christ, be reconciled to God.** (2 Corinthians 15:19, 20)

In Romans, Paul sees reconciliation as a step towards salvation; Christ's death having broken down the enmity between God and man, salvation is "much more"; being reconciled "we shall *be saved* by his life" (5:5-10). Paul's ministry of reconciliation was "Be reconciled to God"; that was his appeal to *the individual*. Reconciliation is one part of the great Salvation obtained for all men by Christ's death in man's place. And it is offered freely to all individuals to accept or reject. But reconciliation, particularly as portrayed in Romans (an Acts epistle), and relevant to God's purpose for the earth, has another aspect, one that involved Israel and the nations and their relationship to God, and to each other.

It was a reversal of God's judgement upon the people (later defined as "the nations") who rebelled against God at the tower of Babel. A rebellion that led to God's choice of Israel as the one "nation" to bring to fulfilment His purpose for the earth and its peoples. At Babel the nations were 'given up by God'; Paul's ministry of reconciliation reversed that position.

Reconciliation: National

Genesis 11 marks a watershed in the purpose of God for the earth. There was a rebellion of the people against God and His command. Given originally to Adam and repeated to Noah, it was, "Be fruitful and multiply and *fill the earth*" (Genesis 1:28; 9:1). But the migrating people determined, having found a fertile plain, to settle down permanently, contrary to God's command. They began to build a city and a tower (probably as a centre of worship).

This "tower" may well have marked the beginnings of idolatry referred to in Romans 1:18-32, where the apostle refers back to those who "exchanged the glory of the immortal God for images resembling mortal man and birds and animals and creeping things" (Romans 1:23).

And so God's judgment fell upon them; he dispersed them and confused their "one language" so that "they could not understand one another's speech". The people left off building the city, and it came to be called Babel, which in later times became Babylon, a symbol of that anti-God system of idolatry whose demise is spoken of in the end times (Genesis 11:7-9; Revelation chapter 18).

This descent of the nations into idolatry and its handmaiden, perversion, is three times said of these people, "God gave them up" (Romans 1:24, 26, 28). And, it was at this point that God chose one man, and one nation (Israel) to effect His purpose for the earth. Through Abraham and his seed all peoples on earth would be blessed (Genesis 2:1-3). Israel were to become God's vessel through which His salvation for all men would be dispensed (John 4:22; Acts 13:46, 47).

But when the Messiah came to make that salvation possible, Israel, nationally, failed to respond. Only a remnant accepted Jesus as Messiah, the majority rejected Him. And so God now turned to the Gentiles, who, whilst God had been preparing Israel to be God's channel of salvation, had been allowed to "walk in their own ways". Now, because of Israel's "failure", God's salvation was extended to the Gentiles. It was "the *reconciliation of the world*".

Paul refers to this in his address to the idolaters in Lystra, when he says, "In past generations God allowed all the nations to walk in their own ways. Yet He did not leave Himself without witness" (Acts 14:16, 17). And in Athens, a place of many idols (17:22-31 please read), he referred back to these "times of ignorance". **But now,** these words (spoken in the middle Acts period) mark a significant change in God's dealing with the nations. With the continuing rejection by the nation of Israel of Jesus as Messiah, Paul announces the reconciliation of the Gentiles. Israel's "rejection" means *the reconciliation of the world*" (Romans 11:13-15).

But when Paul wrote Romans, this did not mark the end of Israel and God's earthly purpose through them. That was not announced until about three years later, when he applied the prophecy of Isaiah (6:9, 10) to the current generation, and declared, "The *salvation of God* has been sent to the Gentiles; they will listen" (Acts 28:25-28). And that "salvation", associated now on with a purpose in the heavenly places, he made known in his prison epistles, Ephesians and Colossians.

5. Redemption

From reconciliation we move to redemption. And we are fortunate in having a picture of just what this is in the experience of Israel and their deliverance from Egypt. In the Song of Moses, that rejoiced in that deliverance, the people sang, "The Lord is my strength and my song, and he has become my salvation ... You have led in your steadfast love the people you have *redeemed*" (Exodus 15:2, 13). This event became a byword in the history of Israel and the Lord reminded them of it when He identified Himself to them as, "I am the Lord your God, *who brought you out* of the house of slavery ... out of the land of Egypt" (Exodus 20:2; Psalm 81:10). Israel's God was a God of redemption and deliverance.

In Biblical times a slave could be 'redeemed' and become a free man by the payment of a ransom, and even in the history of war generally it was common practice to take hostages with the object of receiving payment of a 'ransom' to release them back to their own people. In fact almost anything, property, goods etc., could be 'redeemed' 'at a price' (compare the modern pawnbroker).

The Hebrew word *gaal* (to redeem) has an underlying meaning of *kinship*. It is used in Ruth 3:13 of Boaz who was to "do the part of a kinsman", *redeeming* a parcel of land that belonged to her father-in-law who had since died (chapter 4). And it underlies the redemption of Israel from Egypt insofar that the Lord identified Himself with them saying to Pharaoh, "Let *my people* go" (Exodus 7:16). In typical terms, the Lord's *kinship* with Israel points forward to the *kinship* of Jesus Christ, who identified Himself with man generally, "born in the likeness of men ... found in human form" (Philippians 2:5-8), and Israel specifically, "from *their race, according to the flesh*"—"He came to his own people" (John 1:11; Romans 9:5):

> Since therefore the children share in flesh and blood, He Himself likewise partook of the same things ... He had to be made like His brothers in every respect ... (Hebrews

2:14-17)

Redemption in the New Testament is the Greek *agorazo, exagorazo* and *lutrosis* and cognates. *Agorazo* is 'to buy', and indicates that a 'cost' is involved. Redemption inevitably meant that somebody had to pay. And the One who paid the ultimate cost of our redemption was Christ, who did so at the 'cost' of the shedding of His own blood for us. This is acknowledged in the new song of the 24 elders as they fall down in worship of the Lamb:

> The 24 elders fell down before the Lamb ... they sang a new song ... 'Worthy are you ... for you were slain, and *by your blood you ransomed (agorazo) people for God.'* (Revelation 5:8, 9)

Apolutrosis (redemption) means to release on payment of a ransom. It is used twice in Romans. In 3:23-25 we read, "all have sinned and fall short of the glory of God... justified by grace as a gift, through the *redemption* that is in Christ Jesus... to be received by faith". In 8:23 it refers to the future *"redemption* of our bodies" and is linked to the *setting free* of the whole creation from "its bondage to corruption". So it is a present reality and a future hope.

The Lord summarised His coming and ministry when he said,

> "The Son of man... came to serve, and to give his life as a ransom (*lutron*) for many." (Mark 10:45)

And *The New Bible Dictionary* summed up the meaning of redemption:

> It is the price paid *to release* the slave and to *let* the condemned *go free.* (my italics)

Having now looked at three of the seven words associated with the meaning of salvation, this might be a good place to observe how the different words within the overall concept of salvation are associated with different aspects of the one great sacrifice for mankind. I set them out in structural form.

A Identification with Christ and His sinless life

  B Reconciliation at one with God. The goal, likeness and image

   C Redemption deliverance from sin by His blood

    D Justification He is just and the Justifier. Our faith

   C1 Atonement forgiveness of sins not without blood

  B1 Sanctification to be like God. Be holy as he is

A1 *Aionion* Life living the life of Christ.

A brief look at this structure shows that **A and A1** both deal with life as it was intended to be before the entrance of sin and death. It is *aionion* (usually translated 'eternal' or 'everlasting') life and awaits us in the future. **B** and *B1* are about being in tune with God, being at one with Him, doing His will, being like Him. **C and *C1*** are both centred on the 'blood of Christ', necessary to 'redeem' and to 'atone'. It deals with 'sin' as a cause and 'sins' as the symptoms; the need for forgiveness. It is pictured in Israel's history by the 'redemption' that delivered them once and for all from Egypt (Passover), and 'atonement', that one day in each year, their *Yom Kippur*, Day of Atonement, when the "sins of the people" were remembered, and when the high priest went into the Holy of Holies, "not without blood" to make atonement for them. But all revolve around **D** where salvation is summed up in one verse of Scripture:

> God's righteousness ... That He might be *just* and the *Justifier* of the one who has faith in Jesus. (Romans 3:26)

The sacrifice of Christ was the means by which the salvation of mankind was effected, without compromising the righteousness of God. God could be seen as 'just' and yet 'justify' sinners; His righteousness could be reckoned to us by faith. This is where we begin in the next chapter.

6. Justification by Faith

In looking at the various aspects of salvation we have so far considered

- Identification.
- Reconciliation and
- Redemption.

We now come to what is probably the word that best defines the basic need and reason for salvation, 'righteousness'. When God created man, evidently not intending him to be just a puppet whose actions were controlled by Him, He made him neither righteous nor unrighteous.

At best our first parents could be described as 'innocent'. They could not be dubbed 'righteous' or 'unrighteous' until they had been tested. An alternative was placed before Adam by the LORD God, that called upon him and his wife to obey or disobey a command not to eat of the tree of the knowledge of good and evil.

By disobeying they became 'unrighteous' (Genesis 2:16, 17; 3:1-19). And so, bringing sin and death into the world (Romans 5:12) there came the need for 'salvation', and the need of a Saviour.

The English words 'just, justify, justification', from the Latin *justus,* and 'right, righteous, righteousness' from the old Saxon *reht,* mean virtually the same thing. In the original Greek this is much more obvious, where the word *dikaios* and its cognates are the basis of all these translations. In the simplest conception they express what is 'right' in contrast to what is 'wrong', by some standard set by an authority. And it almost goes without saying that any 'standard' set by man is lower than the 'standard' demanded by God.

For our first parents it was the LORD's command. And, as Paul tells us in Romans 5:12-21 (see chapter 2) just one man's sin (unrighteous act) led to the whole human race needing salvation. And that salvation is found in "the last Adam", the "second man" (1 Corinthians 15:45, 46).

> He was made sin for us, (He) who knew no sin, that we might be made the *righteousness* of God in Him. (2 Corinthians 5:21 *KJV*)

But it is quite obvious that we have not automatically *become* righteous. We might be leading better lives since believing in Him, as we should be (Ephesians 4:1-3; Colossians 3:1-4), but we are still vulnerable and liable to sin; perfection has not yet been reached. But that is how we see ourselves; how does God see us?

This is where the great doctrine of 'justification by faith alone without the works of the law', comes into the equation. It forms an important part of Paul's epistles to the Romans and Galatians, particularly Romans where there are over 60 occurrences to '*dikaios*' and its cognates. God may not have *made us* 'righteous' when we became Christians, but in His sight, and *by His 'reckoning' we can be viewed as such.* Romans chapters 3 & 4 are devoted to man's need of righteousness, how God effected this and how it has been made available to all in Christ, whilst God Himself remains just. In short it is because He accepts our faith in Christ *as a means for* reckoning us to be righteous.

So what in essence is "justification by faith"? On God's side it involves His righteousness; and for the individual, his response—faith. Paul sets it out in Romans 3:23-26. I quote it in the *Moffatt* translation of these verses as the best and simplest I have come across (even so, please read slowly):

> All have sinned and come short of the glory of God, but they are justified for nothing by his grace through the ransom provided in Christ Jesus, whom God put forward as the means of propitiation by his blood, to be received by faith. This was to demonstrate the justice of God in view of the fact that sins previously committed during the time of God's forbearance had been passed over;

it was to demonstrate his justice at the present (time), showing that God is just Himself and that He justifies man on the score of faith in Jesus.

Paul begins with the basic problem, "all have sinned". Earlier he had put it another way—" none is righteous, no, not one" (3:10; Psalm 14:1-3). He then describes God's response to this failure; His forbearance of "sins previously committed" and the means whereby they were "passed over" without compromising His own righteousness—" the ransom provided in Christ Jesus", who was "put forward as *the means of the propitiation* by His blood". But it had to be "received by faith in Jesus". So, not only was man justified, but so also was God, whose righteousness had not been compromised. He had not simply dismissed sin, but had paid its price (its wages) in Jesus, who was a "propitiation" for sin by means of His blood, "for the wages of sin is death" (6:23).

When writing about this great act of justification by faith on God's part, Paul sets it in a context of

Jewish law and in relationship to Abraham, both in Romans (chapters 3 & 4) and Galatians (chapters 2 & 3). That is because both of these epistles were written during the Acts period, when the "hope of the twelve tribes", "the hope of Israel", was still possible of fulfilment (Acts 26:6, 7; 28:20). This was an *earthly* 'hope' based upon the LORD's original promise to Abraham involving the blessing of all nations (Genesis 12:1-3). And during the Acts period believing Gentiles were reckoned just as much "sons of Abraham", as were believing Jews (Romans 4:16, 17; Galatians 3:7-9). Is that true today?

Also at that time there was a strong Judaizing element that tried to insist that believing Gentiles should be circumcised and keep the law of Moses in order to be saved. They did not see why the *status quo* should be abandoned; if Gentiles were to share in Israel's blessings, including salvation, they must also come in the time-honoured way by accepting circumcision and commitment to the Law. This claim was not easily dismissed, and a special council was convened in Jerusalem to debate the question (Acts 15:1-30). After all,

Jewish believers were still keeping the law during this period (Acts 21:19-22). Both these factors will be considered in the next chapter in this series.

7. Justification: Dispensational Aspects

In the previous chapter we considered "Justification by faith" as explained by Paul in Romans and Galatians. And the point was made that this truth was presented within the context of the Acts period, when there was a problem with the relationship of the believing Gentiles to the Law of Moses.

Also, all believers were described *at that time* as "sons of Abraham", he being "the father of us all" (Galatians 3:7-9; Romans 4:16, 17). Is that still true today?

Thankfully, neither of these two matters affect the great truth of "Justification by faith alone", and today the question of Gentiles believers' relationship to the Law of Moses is generally not a problem. However, there are still those who believe that members of the Church, the Body of

Christ are "sons of Abraham" and are blessed under the promise that the LORD gave to Abraham concerning the nations.

Gentiles and the Law of Moses

Some Pharisees amongst the early believers, insisted that to be saved, believing Gentiles should be circumcised and keep the Law of Moses (Acts 15:5). This claim was not easily dismissed, and it was causing quite a bit of confusion and hostility, so a special council was convened in Jerusalem to debate the question (Acts 15:6-30).

Paul and Barnabas and Peter gave testimony, and James, who held a position of authority in the church there, made his judgement. This was that the need for circumcision and law keeping were ruled out as a means to salvation. Christian Jews would continue to be "zealous for the law" (Acts 21:20), but only four "necessary things" must be kept by the Gentiles, things that might offend Jews and prevent them from having fellowship with Christian Gentiles. These are listed in 15:20.

Even so, the problem of the circumcision of Gentile believers never really went away (Acts 21:21), as the later epistle to the Roman church demonstrates.

Sons of Abraham

In Romans chapter 4 Paul refers his readers to the Hebrew Scriptures concerning Abraham and his faith. He does so to establish the fact that Abraham was justified by faith *before* he received the rite of circumcision; he was in fact *effectively a Gentile at the time*. Circumcision was but "a seal of the righteousness that he had by faith *while he was still uncircumcised*" (Romans 4:11). And the purpose of this was "to make Him the father of *all who believe* (Jew and Gentile), so that righteousness would be reckoned to them as well", whether they were circumcised or not (4:9-12). Hence, he established that *all believers* were justified by faith, quite independently of circumcision. But he went further. He went on to say that all believers *at that time* could claim Abraham as their father.

There are two issues here that should be noted. Salvation, proceeding from reconciliation, and including justification, redemption and forgiveness of sins, is *by faith alone*. And this transcends all dispensations (Ephesians 1:7; 2:8; Philippians 3:9 etc.). But is it still true today that Abraham is "the father of all who believe" (4:11)? In Romans Paul links this relationship to the ancient promise made to Abraham—" I have made you the father of many nations" (4:17). He also makes this link to Abraham in Galatians 3:7-9:

> The Scripture, foreseeing that God would justify the Gentiles by faith, *preached the gospel beforehand to Abraham*, saying, "In you shall all nations be blessed". So then, those who are of faith are blessed along with Abraham, the man of faith.

Both Romans and Galatians were written during the Acts period, when Abraham's seed were still in a position to be a blessing to the nations, for in both cases Paul refers "justification by faith" back to that ancient promise that "in Abraham all the families of the earth shall be blessed" (Genesis 12:1-3; 17:5, Romans 4:13, 17; Galatians 4:8, 9). So Gentile believers during Acts could claim Abraham as their father, insofar that they were a kind of firstfruits of this promise, but can we do so today?

Is this what the "gospel" is about today and are our spiritual blessings coming upon the nations through a saved and commissioned Israel today? Can we relate the Abrahamic promise with its earthly 'hope' to the spiritual blessings in the heavenly places of the Body of Christ? It would hardly seem so. It is one thing to see Abraham as *an example* of justification by faith, but our 'hope' is neither national nor is it to be realised on earth. To emphasise the difference between the situation during Acts and the situation today, consider Paul's picture of The Olive Tree in Romans 11.

Christians during the Acts period were described as either the "natural branches" (Jews), or "wild shoots" (Gentiles) "grafted into" the Olive tree of Israel (chapter 11). Here, as everywhere else in the epistle, whilst there is no difference between the two as regards "justification by faith", in every other respect the Jew was "first" (1:16; 2:9, 10. It was an "advantage" in being a Jew (3:1, 2) and they had *a sevenfold privilege* over the Gentile (9:4, 5) etc. The Olive Tree sums up that difference describing Jews as "natural branches" and Gentiles as "wild shoots". Can we truly describe the situation today in those terms? Gentiles "shared in the nourishing root of the olive tree". Where is the Olive Tree today?

It seems evident that when Paul pronounced judgement upon the nation of Israel (Acts 28:25-28), not only did "the hope of Israel" go into abeyance, but the Olive Tree was cut down. If the unfulfilled prophecies in both the Old and New Testaments are to be believed, then that tree will grow again, and God will again take up His purpose for the earth through them. But in the meanwhile, another 'hope' has been revealed (Ephesians, Colossians) that does not rely on the promises to Abraham concerning the nations, nor the salvation of the nation of Israel. Within that 'hope' we can rejoice that we are also justified by faith, even though we are not "sons of Abraham", nor reliant on a saved Israel.

8. Atonement

As we continue to look at the different aspects of the great salvation we have in Christ, made possible by His sacrifice, "once and for all", we have reached Atonement. In chapter 2 in this series, we saw how 'Identification in Christ' dealt with Adam's *one* sin; 'Atonement' deals with man's *many sins, and their forgiveness*. In both the Old and New Testaments it is provided for a redeemed people. God accounted Israel as a redeemed nation, and gave to them the means to atone for their many sins as individuals. But it came at a cost:

> Under the law almost everything is purified with blood, and *without the shedding of blood there is no forgiveness of sins.* (Hebrews 9:22)

And that marked the need for the One Great Sacrifice, made once for all, the anti-type of the sacrifice made, "not without the shedding of blood", on Israel's Day of Atonement, but as we shall see effective for all peoples.

"Atonement", (Hebrew *kaphar* and *kopher*), occur together in Genesis 6:14 *KJV* where Noah is told by God to make an ark of gopher wood and "pitch (*kaphar*) it within and without with pitch (*kopher*)". Hence its original meaning is 'to cover or shelter'. The cognate *kapporeth* is the name of the "mercy seat" (Exodus 25:17). This was the lid of the Ark of the Covenant within which the Law of God was kept. As the people of Israel move around, so the Tabernacle containing the ark travelled with them, and later the Ark of the Covenant was kept in the Temple.

Once a year, on The Day of Atonement, and out of sight of all the people, the High Priest went alone into the Most Holy Place of all and made sacrifice for the sins of the nation, by sprinkling the lid of the ark (the mercy seat) with blood. This day is known as *Yom Kippur,* and it was the most solemn day in Israel's calendar. On this day of repentance and "solemn rest", Israel were commanded, "afflict yourselves". On this day, the sins of the past year were remembered.

Failing to recognising this solemn day, or to work on it, was punished by being cut off from the people and death. It was "a Day of Atonement, *to make atonement* for (Israel) before the LORD". And it was a "statute for ever throughout your generations in all your dwelling places" (Leviticus 23:26-32). This great day will have its anti-type at the return of the LORD to the Mount of Olives, when:

> Every eye will see Him, even those who pierced Him, and *all the tribes of the land (ge) will wail (mourn)* on account of Him. (Revelation 1:7, see Zechariah 12:10-14; 14:1-4).

The passage in Revelation must be interpreted by the passages in Zechariah. Whilst this great event will not of course be kept secret from the rest of the world, the Messiah is coming primarily to Israel, looked at in terms of the twelve tribes. And when He comes, and they see Him, the effect upon this people who now realise that it was they "who pierced Him", is a great mourning; a mourning as great as that memorable occasion in Israel's history when good king Josiah, king of Judah, was shot by Egyptian archers and died from his wounds (2 Chronicles 35:20-27). This answers to the "affliction" demanded by the LORD, on *Yom Kippur* (Leviticus 23:26-28).

During the Acts period, following the Messiah's first coming, Israel were being called to repentance as a nation (2:14, 36-38), but only a 'remnant' responded (Romans 11:5-7, 25). A future generation, however, will respond, a generation of Israel on earth at the time of the Lord's return as prophesied in the above Scriptures, and they will have their *Yom* Kippur; mourning as they look upon the One they pierced. But this time, He comes "not to deal with sin but to save those who are eagerly waiting for Him" (Hebrews 9:28).

In Hebrews chapters 9 &10, the writer sees the ritual on the Day of Atonement as a type of Christ's work of atonement for His people; "the blood of calves and goats" finding their anti-type in the sacrifice of Christ Himself (9:19-26). That one great sacrifice of Christ, just as it was on *Yom Kippur* was collective, for all people. But unlike *Yom Kippur,* it did not need to be repeated:

> He has appeared *once for all* at the end of the ages *to put away sin by the sacrifice of Himself.* (Hebrews 9:26); 10:1-7)

But Hebrews associates this "single offering" with a New Covenant, contrasting it with the old covenant of Law. Both covenants were made with Israel and Judah (Jeremiah 31:31-34; Hebrews 8:1-12; 10:14-18). I will come to the significance of this and its relationship to the Church, the Body of Christ in a later chapter (number 11). Here, I want to emphasise that whilst atonement is presented in Hebrews in relation to Israel, it is just as much part of the salvation that God offers to all people today.

In the wider spectrum of the atoning work of Christ, we today in the Body of Christ can also praise God in that, the blood of Christ was given for our sakes also. And it is equally effective in covering our sins. Although the word "atonement" (Greek *katallage, katallasso*) does not occur in the two great epistles that outline the blessings of the Church today (Ephesians, Colossians), this aspect of salvation follows the same pattern as it did in Israel's history. It is enshrined in 'the Charter of the Church' (Ephesians 1:3-14) where it follows redemption:

> In (Christ) we have redemption through His blood, *the forgiveness of sins* according to the riches of His grace, which He lavished upon us. (Ephesians 1:7)

We do not have a Day of Atonement once a year, but we can rejoice in "the forgiveness of sins" associated with it. Just as Israel were first 'redeemed', delivered from slavery in Egypt, and then, as a redeemed nation, were forgiven their sins, so we are told that, in Christ, not only do we have "redemption through his blood", but "the forgiveness of sins". And all by His grace, lavished upon us, and "to the praise of his glory" (1:6, 12, 14).

9. Sanctification

In this series we have so far looked at five aspects of the great salvation we have in Christ Jesus;

- Identification,
- Reconciliation,
- Redemption,
- Justification and
- Atonement.

These all speak of what God in Christ did to 'restore' humanity to what it was intended to be before the entrance of sin and death into the world. Made in the likeness of the image of God, man was intended to be "like Christ", which we will be at some future day:

Beloved, we are God's children now, and what we will be has not yet appeared; but we know that when he appears *we shall be like Him*, because we shall see Him as He is. (1 John 3:2) Such a goal is in view for all God's people, and it was just such a temptation that the serpent set before Eve that seemed to offer this, possibly as 'a short cut', but, in the words of the serpent:

"You will be like God (gods) ..." (Genesis 3:5).

The consequences of this led to the need for the salvation expressed in those five great words referred to above. But 'salvation' as understood in both the Old and New Testaments, is more than 'restoration' of something lost. It involves both the life lived now and that which is to come, and hence we now move on to Sanctification and *Aionion* Life. In this chapter I am looking at the first of these, that speaks of *how we live our present life*, in our present bodies, and what God requires of us taking into consideration our weaknesses. I begin by looking at the typical people, Israel, and what the LORD required of them.

Be holy as I am holy

The Lord commanded Israel:

"I am the *LORD* your God, *consecrate yourselves* therefore, and *be holy, for I am holy* ... I am the *LORD* who brought you up out of the land of Egypt to be your God. You shall therefore *be holy, for I am holy.*" (Leviticus 11:44,45)

Following their redemption, Israel were called to holiness. Reminding them constantly of that *deliverance*, even in the way He describes Himself, "the *LORD* who brought you up out of the land of Egypt", He now calls for the logical outcome of that redemption, *therefore*, "Be holy, for I the LORD am holy". Be like me. And this is relevant not just for Israel at this time, but also for all God's people of every hope and calling.

In Israel's case that 'holiness' was both corporate and individual. Subject to their obedience and by keeping the LORD's covenant they, as a nation, could be: "My treasured possession among all peoples, for all the earth is mine; *and you shall be to me* a kingdom of priests and *a holy nation.* (Exodus 19:5, 6). But national holiness is dependent upon individual holiness, and no generation of Israel has yet attained that status. The history of Israel recorded in the Acts of the Apostles, is yet another example of their failure in this respect. But the unfulfilled prophecies concerning Israel show that they will attain it one day. On an individual basis, however, all God's people are called to holiness. So what is holiness? Andrew Bonar wrote in his *Commentary on Leviticus*:

> Holiness is the Lord's design and aim. He longs to have His creature freed from all uncleanliness, and made holy. He seeks to hear on earth no longer the cry of wickedness and woe, but the blissful cry that seraph utters to seraph, "Holy, holy, holy". (See Isaiah 6:1-3)

We associate a number of words with holiness; sanctification, consecration, purity, hallowing, reverence, piety, devotion, dedication etc. In the Scriptures sanctification and holiness are generally translations of the Hebrew *qodash/ qadosh* and the Greek *hagios / heiros*. Derived from these words we also have, temple (with its

Holy place and Holiest of all), priest(hood), and saint (holy person) as used by Paul in his letter to the Roman church (1:7). The fundamental meaning of *hagios* is "separation, and so to speak, consecration and devotion to the service of Deity" (Trench *Synonyms*). It is the word most used in the New Testament and the Greek translation of the Hebrew Bible from which Paul often quoted.) This aspect of 'separation' was particularly relevant to Israel *as a nation apart* (Leviticus 20:24), and on an individual basis has its place today, not by withdrawing from the world, but by being, **in** the world but not **of** the world, as the Lord prayed to His Father concerning His disciples:

> They are not of the world, just as I am not of the world. *Sanctify* (*hagiazo*) them in the truth, your word is truth. You have sent me into the world, so I have sent them into the world. And for their sake I *sanctify* (*hagiazo*) myself, that they also may be *sanctified* (*hagiazo*) in truth. (John 17:16-19)

Sanctification here is associated with God's word of truth, just as it was in Israel's case with obeying the LORD's commandments. In Paul's words, "Let *the word of Christ* dwell in you richly" (Colossians 3:16). It is not hiding ourselves away from the world but living "the Truth" *whilst in it*. Seen in practical terms Paul wrote in Romans 6:19-22:

> Just as you once presented your members as slaves to impurity ... so now present your members as slaves to righteousness *leading to sanctification* (*hagiasmos*) ... you have been set free from sin and have become slaves to God, *the fruit you get leads to sanctification* (*hagiasmos*) and its end, eternal (*aionion*) life.

Rest on the redemption God has given you in Christ; no longer slaves to sin, but as freemen, and yet "slaves (servants) to God". The "fruit you get" is described for us in Galatians 5:22,23: "love, joy, peace, patience, kindness, goodness, faithfulness, gentleness, self-control". It is the "fruit of the Spirit" produced by those who "belong to Christ" and who "walk by the Spirit" (verses 24-25). And that fruit "leads to sanctification". Sanctification is achieved, not by just receiving salvation by grace, but *grasping* the abundance of that grace and taking hold of life in Christ. We have been identified with Christ, reckon it to be so (Romans 5, chapter 3).

10. *Aionion* Life

I have spoken of *aionion* life in this series, to express that life which has been promised to those who believe in Jesus Christ. This is because there is no agreement amongst scholars and commentators as to its meaning. There are four main views on the subject.

1) The popular view, and that which probably most of us were brought up on, is that it is everlasting, eternal, life without end. This is supported by the statement that "the last enemy to be destroyed is death" (1 Corinthians 15:26) and that in the New Jerusalem, that comes down to the new earth, "death shall be no more" (Revelation 21:4). Also the promise that "this mortal body must put on immortality" (1 Corinthians 15:53-55).

2) Those who recognise that underlying the Greek there is the suggestion of ages,

rather than eternity. Hence we get renderings of Romans 6:22 for example, "life age-during" (*Young's Literal Translation*) and "the Life of the Ages" (*Weymouth's New Testament in Modern Speech*). C.H. Welch in *Alphabetical Analysis* Part 1 states that "Eternity is **not** a Biblical theme".

3) Since the Greek *aion* in the Septuagint (Greek Old Testament) is the usual translation of the Hebrew *olam, Brown-Driver-Briggs* give the primary meaning of *olam*, as "long duration, antiquity, futurity".

4) *The Companion Bible* Appendix 151, says that the Hebrew *olam* "is derived from *alam* (to hide) and means the hidden time or age, like *aion*", and *aionion* is "belonging to an age".

So, summarising; *aionion* life may be life without end; life enjoyed through a number of ages, however many there may be. Perhaps it is a way of expressing a very long time in the future, or maybe it is a way of saying it is at present something *hidden* from us. In respect of this last I recall Colossians 3:3, 4: "Your life is *hidden with Christ in God.* When Christ who is your life appears, then you also will appear with Him in glory". On my part, I am happy to rest upon the 'hope' expressed in this passage in Colossians. And, although John was writing to people with a different 'hope', his words in 1 John 1:1, 2 *NRSV* are very significant:

> We declare to you ... what we have heard, what we have seen with our eyes, what we have looked at and touched with our hands, concerning the word of life ... the *aionion* life that was with the Father and was revealed to us.

John, referring to the One who was with the Father, seen and heard by the disciples and touched with their hands; the One they recognised as the Messiah—He **is** *aionion* life. He said Himself, "I am the way and the truth and *the life*" (John 14:6). Looked at in this way, we cannot visualise an end to that life, it is the life of Christ.

Perhaps, rather than dwelling on *aionion life* in respect of how long it is, we should concentrate more on its *nature*, for I believe that in some respects we can already enter into that life. Paul wrote:

> I have been crucified with Christ. It is no longer I that live, but Christ who lives in me. And the life I now live in the flesh I live by faith in the Son of God, who loved me and gave Himself for me. (Galatians 2:20)

And the Lord speaking to the Jews during His earthly ministry, said, "Truly, truly, I say to you, whoever hears my word and believes Him who sent me *has eternal life*. He does not come into judgement, but *has passed from death to life"* (John 5:24). Not will at some future date, but has already passed to *aionion* life. Paul throws light on how this works in practice when he writes in Romans 6:1-14, that if we are identified with

Christ in His death and resurrection, then, although this does not appear outwardly to be so, for we still have the same sinful body, we should account (or reckon) that it is so. "Present yourselves to God *as those who have been brought from death to life*" (verse 13; see chapter 3).

Looking specifically at *aionion* life in relation to the Church which is the Body of Christ, it is only mentioned in the Pastoral Epistles. In the Old Testament it is found only in Daniel 12:2, which together with the other New Testament references, all deal with God's purpose for the earth. How much we should read into this is a matter of opinion, and enforces my suggestion that we should concentrate more on the *nature* of our life in Christ, rather than how long it will last. And that takes us back to the previous chapter in this series, Sanctification.

We do know however that it is life that will be enjoyed by God's people, Jews and Gentiles, in different environments; the new earth, the heavenly Jerusalem and the heavenly places. But wherever we enjoy "the things that God has prepared for those who love Him" (1 Corinthians 2:9) we know that none of it would have been possible without the great Salvation, with its many facets, procured at great cost by the Jewish Messiah and the Gentiles' Christ, Jesus, "the Lamb of God, who takes away the sin of the world" (John 1:29).

The first occurrence of *olam* in the Scriptures follows Adam's disobedience, when the Lord seems to express His horror at the thought of sinful beings living *for ever*:

> The Lord God said, "Behold, the man has become like one of us in knowing good and evil. Now, lest he reach out his hand and take also of the tree of life and eat, and live *for ever* (*olam*)"—therefore the Lord God sent him out from the garden of Eden to work the ground from which he was taken. (Genesis 3:22, 23)

Adamic life, based upon being 'in Adam', cannot be "for ever", it must, as Adam was warned, lead to death. *Aionion* life is in Christ and hence I cannot see that it can be subject to the end of any age. According to where it will be enjoyed it may be different in 'kind' according to the environment in which one is blessed, but if it is in Christ, then it is secure.

11. The New Covenant and the Church (part 1)

In the previous chapters we have looked at seven aspects of the great salvation that God has provided for man in Christ Jesus; Identification, Reconciliation, Redemption, Justification, Atonement, Sanctification and *Aionion* Life. It would be wrong to imagine that those seven words exhaust the subject; we have in fact only just touched the surface of this great truth. And one aspect of God's redemption that I believe is important is The New Covenant. This is especially so, since much of Christian worship revolves round it. It is important to see The New Covenant in the context of the Scriptures as a whole, especially its relationship to Israel to whom the Old Covenant of Law was given. David's prayer before the LORD, recorded in 1 Chronicles 17 states the position of Israel in God's eyes:

There is none like you, O LORD, and there is no God beside you ... And who is like your people Israel, the one nation on earth whom God went to redeem to be his people ... you made your people Israel to be your people for ever, and you, O LORD, became their God. (1 Chronicles 17:20-22)

This permanence of Israel promised by God, appears again in the context of The New Covenant in Jeremiah 31:31-34, that is followed by this declaration of intent:

Thus says the LORD, who gives the sun for light by day and the fixed order of the moon and stars for light by night ... "If this fixed order departs from before me, declares the LORD, then shall the offspring of Israel cease from being a nation before me for ever". (Jeremiah 31:35, 36)

An interpretation that first appeared in writing (A.D. 160) in Justin Martyr's *Dialogue with Trypho* (*the Jew*), claimed that Christians had replaced Israel in God's eyes, they were the new, spiritual Israel, and that the Jewish Scriptures were theirs, because they kept them. This interpretation has persisted throughout the ages of Christendom, preached as truth from the pulpit, even appearing in many hymns still sung today. The above two passages demonstrate that identification of the present 'Church' as a 'spiritual' Israel, taking the place of Israel, the "(LORD's) people for ever", cannot be correct. But, however innocent this view may seem to be, it has led to a misunderstanding concerning The New Covenant.

The New Covenant

Set out at length in both Jeremiah 31:31-34 (Old Testament) and Hebrews 8:7-12 (New Testament) it clearly looks back to, and contrasts it with, the LORD's covenant of Law made with Israel in the time of Moses.

> Behold, the days are coming, declares the LORD, when I will make a new covenant with the house of Israel and with the house of Judah, *not like the covenant that I made*

with their fathers on the day when I took them by the hand to bring them out of the land of Egypt, my covenant that they broke ... this is the covenant that I will make with the house of Israel after those days, declares the LORD: I will put my law within them, and I will write it on their hearts. And I will be their God, and they shall be my people.

The Gospel period ended with the Messiah ratifying this covenant in His own blood. Referring to His coming death He said at the Last Supper—" This cup that is poured out for you is the new covenant in my blood". But that death not only ratified The New Covenant, but, from a human point of view, it represented Israel's rejection of their Messiah. And to reject the Author of that covenant, was to reject its possible fulfilment, *at that time.*

However, it was not the end for that generation of Israel, they were given a second chance. From the cross the Messiah cried:

"Father, *forgive them*, for they know not what they do." (Luke 23:34)

And following the resurrection, Peter speaking to his own people, said of the crucifixion, "And now brothers, I know that *you acted in ignorance*, as did your rulers ... Repent therefore, and turn again... that he may send the Messiah appointed for you..." (Acts 3:17-20). The Acts story is the record of that 'second chance', but it is also the story of Israel's continuing intransigence, ending in their judgement and rejection (Acts 28:25-28). So where now was The New Covenant made with Israel, now rejected by God as a nation?

During the Acts period a letter was written to Hebrew believers (possibly also encompassing doubters and unbelievers) in which the relationship of this covenant to the then present time was made clear. Urging them not to "neglect such a great salvation", the writer, comparing the two covenants, old and new, said:

In speaking of a new covenant, (God)

makes the first one obsolete. And what is *becoming obsolete* and *growing old* is *ready to vanish away*. (Hebrews 2:3; 8:13)

What the writer does **not** say is that the new has actually, *at that time*, replaced the old. It is ready to, but something is holding it up. And that 'something' was Israel's repentance and recognition of Jesus as Messiah. This was the message that was proclaimed during that period (Acts 3:17-26; 9:22; 17:1-3; 18:28). And John wrote a Gospel with the same intent, "these are written so that you may believe that Jesus is the Messiah" (20:30,31). But, as I said above, reject the Author and you reject the covenant. And so The New Covenant went into abeyance to await a future day and a future generation. So what now?

I believe that this subject has been at times presented in such a way that what I have drawn attention to above has been misunderstood. The fact that The New Covenant may not have been in operation during the Acts period (believers may have had 'a taste' of conditions associated with it *at that time*, Hebrews 6:4, 5), and is not in operation today, is not the end of 'salvation'. The One great sacrifice of Christ and the salvation it offers to everyone, is not confined to The New Covenant. Just as 'justification by faith' was not reliant on circumcision and the keeping of the law, neither is 'salvation' dependent on being under The New Covenant. The redemption accomplished by "the blood of Christ" encompasses *more than* The New Covenant, and I will come to this in the next chapter.

12. The New Covenant and the Church (part 2)

In the previous chapter, I considered The New Covenant, what it was and to whom it was given. I concluded by noting that The New Covenant, just like 'justification by faith' which was not reliant on circumcision and the keeping of the law, so 'salvation' is not dependent on being under The New Covenant. The redemption accomplished by "the blood of Christ" encompasses *more than* The New Covenant, and in this chapter I want to show that this is so, according to the Scriptures. The Church which is the Body of Christ, whilst it owes its very existence to the sacrifice of Christ and the 'salvation' that is offered to all people, is not dependent upon a covenant that 'replaced' an old covenant made with all Israel. The New Covenant was promised to the same people who were under the Old Covenant of Law. It was promised when they were a divided kingdom, "the house of Israel and the house of Judah" (Jeremiah 31:31-34; Hebrews 8:8-13).

Writing towards the end of the Acts period, Paul spoke of Israel's priority and the privileges they still enjoyed *at that time*, and listing those privileges he wrote of,

> My brethren, my kinsmen according to the flesh. They are Israelites, and to them belong the adoption, the glory, *the covenants,* the giving of the law, the worship and the promises. To them belong the patriarchs, and from their race, according to the flesh, is the Christ. (Romans 9:3-5)

Included amongst Israel's privileges was, "to them ... the covenants". This was Israel's position during the late-Acts period; all the covenants belonged to them. (The covenants made with Noah are not included because Israel, as such, did not exist at the time). And so it was with The New Covenant; it was made with "the house of

Israel and the house of Judah". It was not operational during the Acts period, since, although it had been ratified by the blood of Christ, that generation of Israel were not ready for it, as history testifies. They showed no evidence that the LORD's law was "within them" or that it was "written on their hearts" (Jeremiah 31:33), and they rejected their Messiah. Hence The New Covenant awaits the return of the LORD to another generation of that people (Zechariah 14:4; Acts 1:11; Revelation 1:7).

The Church, the Body of Christ

So what relation does the 'Church' have to these things? Christendom has built its worship around the belief that it is under The New Covenant, even though it shows no signs of those things which mark it as being in operation (above). And it is only by claiming that it is the new, spiritual Israel that allows Christians to apply this covenant to a mainly Gentile church, that was never under the old covenant of law in the first place. And that identification is only first found in writing nearly 100 years after the death of the apostles Peter and Paul (see the previous chapter 11).

I have no wish in my observations above, to disturb the faith and practice of any Christian. Readers must judge for themselves whether those observations are scriptural or not, and act according to their own consciences (cp. Acts 24:16). But it is only right on my part to draw attention to a greater and higher 'hope and calling' that is the Church's by right and based on the same great sacrifice of Jesus Christ. Consequent upon God's rejection of Israel (Acts 28:20,25-28) and their 'hope' (Acts 26:6,7), and with the promise of The New Covenant going into abeyance, Paul revealed a calling in the heavenly places in his two epistles that followed that rejection—Ephesians and Colossians. These are the 'charter' of today's 'Church', the Church which is the Body of Christ.

In Ephesians 1:3-14 this 'charter' is laid out in detail (please read). In his Commentary on this passage in Ephesians, J. Armitage Robinson wrote:

The twelve verses baffle our analysis. They are a kaleidoscope of dazzling lights and shifting colours.

The passage begins by telling us that we are "blessed in Christ with every spiritual blessing in the heavenly places". These "heavenly places" are associated with where Christ is seated, and where we are seated with Him (2:4-6). This is in stark contrast to the blessings promised under The New Covenant, made with "the house of "Israel" and to be enjoyed on earth, wonderful though they are.

Colossians 3:3 throws some light on this calling in the heavenly places when it says, "your life is hidden with Christ in God. When Christ who is your life appears, then you also will appear with Him in glory". A present fact and a future 'hope', not associated with the Messiah's return to the Mount of Olives on earth or with The New Covenant, but with Christ's appearance in glory. This is the 'hope and calling' that Paul prays his readers "may know" (Ephesians1:16-18), and which he claims later in this letter was "a mystery... made known to me by revelation" (3:3). This mystery can be seen in context when we set out the whole of Ephesians 3:2-7:

- **The mystery:** "If you have heard of the dispensation of the grace of God which is given me toward you, How that *by revelation he made known unto me* **the mystery**, as I wrote before in few words, By which, when you read ..."

- **The mystery of Christ:** "... you may understand my knowledge in **the mystery of Christ**, which *in other ages was not made known* unto the sons of men, *as it is now revealed* unto his holy apostles and prophets by the Spirit ..."

- **The mystery:** "... That the Gentiles should be fellow heirs, and of the same body, and partakers of his promise in Christ by the gospel, of which I was made a minister ..."

(For more on this see the author's *The Mystery of Ephesians,* published by The Open Bible Trust).

In the context of this series of chapters on 'salvation', we read that one of the blessings of the "Church which is the Body of Christ" is:

> In the Beloved (God's Son Jesus Christ) *we have redemption through his blood, the forgiveness of our trespasses*, according to the riches of his grace which he lavished upon us. (verses 6, 7)

Let us rejoice in that redemption and forgiveness as part of God's great salvation in Christ Jesus, revealed especially in Paul's two great Prison Epistles, Ephesians and Colossians, and go on to practice "things that accompany salvation" (Ephesian 4:1-3; cp. Hebrews 6:9 *KJV*):

**Walk in a manner worthy of the calling
to which you have been called,
with all humility and gentleness, with patience,
bearing with one another in love,
eager to maintain the unity of the Spirit.**

****

About the author

Brian Sherring was born in Isleworth, Middlesex, England in 1932. Following a technical education, he took an engineering apprenticeship and worked for some years as a design draughtsman in agricultural engineering. He was one time Assistant Principal of The Chapel of the Opened Book in London and wrote regular articles for *The Berean Expositor* and several booklets. He then spent some 25 years in the food import business and worked with farm animals at weekends as a hobby. He now lives with his wife in retirement in Surrey.

He has written many Bible Study Booklets and four major books:

- *Paul's Letter to the Romans: Background & Introduction*

- *The Mystery of Ephesians*
- *Messiah and His people.*
- *The Ten Commandments*

More information of these four books is given on pages 93-95.

Information about the numerous Bible Study Booklets written by Brian Sherring can be seen on **www.obt.org.uk** (the website of The Open Bible Trust) or you can use this url:

http://www.obt.org.uk/brian-sherring

Free Sample

Brian Sherring is a regular contributor to
***Search* magazine.**

For a free sample of
the Open Bible Trust's magazine *Search*,
please email admin@obt.org.uk or visit

www.obt.org.uk/search

For a full list of books available from
The Open Bible Trust,
please visit

www.obt.org.uk

Also by Brian Sherring

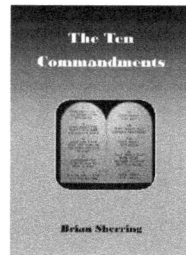

| Paul's Letter to the Romans Background & Introduction | The Mystery of Ephesians | Messiah and His people | The Ten Commandments |

Paul's Letter to the Romans:
Background & Introduction

This book sets Paul's letter to the Romans in the context of both the New Testament and his other letters. It gives the reader a good basis for a detailed study of the epistle.

It was written from Greece some three years before Paul arrived in Rome (Acts 20:2-3). This means that it was written *before* the judgment Paul pronounced upon the Jewish leaders in Rome (Acts 28:25-28). That is *before* Paul wrote Ephesians and Colossians in which new teachings are revealed about a heavenly calling, about Gentile and Jewish equality, and about the aboli*shment of the Law of Moses. It is essential when reading Romans, not to read back into it such teaching as these, and the author does an excellent job of explaining Romans in its correct historical context.

The Mystery of Ephesians

In Ephesians 3:3 Paul mentions a 'mystery', and states that he had written about it briefly, i.e. earlier in the letter. So ... What is this 'mystery'? ... Why have so few Christians heard about it? ... And why do some, who have heard about it, reject it? ... Even oppose it?

With great clarity Brian Sherring explains the Greek word translated 'mystery' does not mean something 'mysterious' but refers to a 'secret', and this 'secret' is an important one. It relates to all mankind, and God had just revealed it to Paul and wanted Paul to make it known far and wide ... which is just what he did in writing Ephesians.

Messiah and His People

In this book Brian Sherring takes the reader through the Bible and the unfolding portrait it paints of the Messiah, the Christ, the Redeemer.

He starts off in Genesis 3, where we learn of the seed of the woman who is to crush the serpent's head, and as we progress through time, slowly more and more is revealed about this One. He is to descend from Abraham and be of the house of David. He is to be born of a virgin and be born in Bethlehem.

He is to combine the offices of Prophet, Priest and King. From Ephesians 1 we learn that in the end He is to be head over all things and Philippians 2 states He is to have that Name which is above every name.

The Ten Commandments

In spite of an increasing lack of knowledge of the Bible in Britain, the Ten Commandments are probably still the best known set of laws in the West. They lie behind our justice system and, in Christian society, form an outline of what God requires of mankind. They are of course, only an outline, or skeleton, that needs to be expanded— and that is just what this book does.

****

The above four are available as perfect bound
paperbacks from
www.obt.org.uk
and from

The Open Bible Trust,
Fordland Mount, Upper Basildon,
Reading, RG8 8LU, UK.

They are also available as
eBooks from Amazon and Apple
and as KDP paperback from Amazon

More on Salvation

Salvation: God Provision and Man's Response
By Brian Sherring

'Salvation' is a word which has slipped out of everyday language. People may talk about 'God' and 'church' but much less is heard about 'being saved'. However, from the looking at the world around us it is clear that mankind has a deep need; a need for peace today and a need for assurance of what is to happen 'afterwards' - i.e. after life has ended.

From its earliest chapters, the Bible speaks of man's great need for 'salvation', and from then on it runs like a golden thread throughout the Bible. However much man may need 'salvation', he can do nothing about it, but we need not despair. It is God who provides it and gives it.

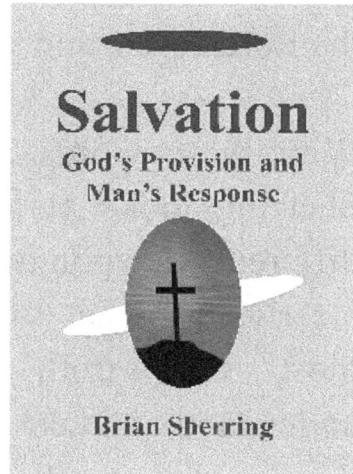

This booklet is, thankfully, not a theological treatise of the subject of 'salvation'. Rather it considers the basic truth of 'salvation' which is enshrined in the words of Acts 16:31: "Believe in the Lord Jesus, and you shall be saved."

With these words as his starting point, Brian Sherring looks at salvation from a number of different viewpoints, enabling the reader to see clearly just what salvation is, and that it is the most vital truth for every individual to understand and take hold of for themselves. Read this booklet, and then pass it on to others.

Salvation: Safe and Secure?
By Sylvia Penny

This important book is a thorough treatment of the subject of salvation, asking such questions as …

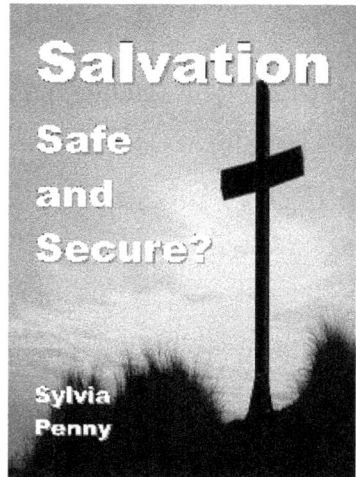

- What is it, exactly, that saves us?
- Is salvation secure?
- Can it be lost?
- What is 'conditional security'?

It deals with a wide number of issues such as …

- Salvation and works
- The doctrine of rewards
- Lordship salvation
- Free grace theology
- Assurance of salvation
- Why people lose their faith

That Wonderful Redemption

By Athol Walter

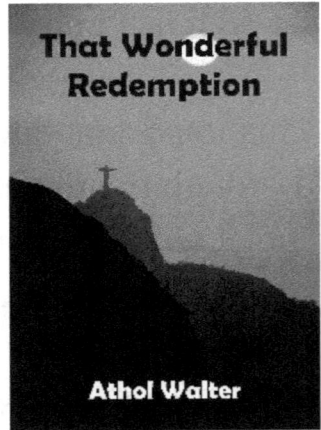

That Wonderful Redemption

Athol Walter

The question the unbeliever should ask is, "What must I do to be saved?" But ... the believer should ask, "What did God have to do in order to save me?"

This book deals mainly with the second question. However, we do not need understand how salvation works in order to be saved. God saves the sinner purely on the basis of faith in the Lord Jesus Christ's sacrifice for sin and His resurrection. But surely a desire to understand and know in part how it works must surely follow.

God's Plan of Salvation is made up of a number of parts, each one being necessary to the success of the whole. Moreover, if any one of the parts is absent or fails, then the whole scheme fails. It is this teaching that underlies what is presented here.

However, it must be said that no matter how much we know or understand how God's wonderful salvation works, we will never fully know it all, never completely understand it all, and will never be able to answer all questions.

Moreover, there comes a time when all the studying and analyzing must stop, and we simply must bow in submission and adoration and appreciation before our great God and Saviour, Jesus Christ.

****

These books are available as paperbacks from
www.obt.org.uk and from

The Open Bible Trust,
Fordland Mount, Upper Basildon,
Reading, RG8 8LU, UK.

They are also available as eBooks
from Amazon and Apple and as
KDP paperback from Amazon

About this book

Seven Aspects of Salvation

In short, but comprehensive, coverage Brian Sherring gives the reader a greater understanding of 'salvation'. We may often use the word 'saved', but having been 'saved' do we appreciate many of the other gracious blessings that goes along with it, such as:

- Identification with Christ
- Reconciliation
- Redemption
- Justification
- Atonement
- Sanctification
- Eternal Life

And, with respect to salvation, what is the role of the New Covenant; (a) with respect to Israel, and (b) with respect to the Church the Body of Christ?

www.ingramcontent.com/pod-product-compliance
Lightning Source LLC
Chambersburg PA
CBHW070529030426
42337CB00016B/2161